STAY NO GO

a story of love & loss

by Jim White

ঐরিকা

পানোজ

For KP:

The inspiration for this book

THE CONTINUOUS
PRESENCE OF ABSENCE

I've tried everything

to stop
this feeling

these thoughts
  keep streaming
  in and out
like ships to port
and back out to sea
  endless waves
  seemingly forever
  under the surface
bobbing up for oxygen
barely able
  to inhale
  exhale
like any moment the air will be popped
  from the balloon.
And yet here I am
once again
  awake with the dawn
and wonder if I'll ever
see you
hear your soothing voice
look into you
oh those deep blue eyes
touch your soft skin

I can't just
  move on

Jim White

like I thought
like they said
I know I need
something
but what?

your absence becoming
presence.

WORDS WITH NO POWER

Move on
  forget about it
get over it
you're gonna be fine
  you deserve to be
  happy
it's over
  you gotta
  you need to
  you should
  why don't you...
all the suggestions
requests
pleading cliches
  amounted to
  nothing
none could help me
  move on
  get over it
  forget
none of their words had any power
no energy
spark
soul

but why?

They didn't come from within
and they have no idea
why
where
when
my spirit will fly
or flee

Jim White

to be
free
in love
with
or without
because there is
no
other.

as hard
as that is
to understand.

THERE IS ONLY ONE

You
Who
I would do
  anything for
  any time of day

Only one
you
who knew
me
like you
who I want to lay down with
after a long day

Only one
you
who I want to kiss
slowly
savoring each moment
like it was the only one
that exists

Only you
  can drive me straight up the wall like this
  flipped upside down, shook up, twisted
wondering how
  I will ever find you
again.

Only you
  who
I still yearn for
in bed
in the truck
at the table

Jim White

on the floor
after all this time
only you.

IT FELT JUST RIGHT

We met on a chilly October night
headlights in view
an open road of possibility
a frozen rear on a park bench
calm cool and chill
smooth as the surface of lake Erie
before us

on our second date you told me your
middle name
we laughed all day
there was something special
about you
a new tingle tangle never experienced before
forces aligned
we took it slow

it felt
just
right.

HOOKED

Her beauty radiates
just as much in a tie-dye and sweats
as a sun dress or yoga pants
just as sexy in jeans and boots or
a bath towel

her beauty spoke in silence
or everyday conversation
when you ache
for the sound of her voice
the embrace
after a day of storms

waiting at the airport
as she walks into view
with backpack and sunshine
that engine hum vibe within
is true
you're hooked on the real deal
nothing compares
to that feel.

WITH ME, ALWAYS

I'm reaching for
anything
that will shut off
    my mind
    emotions
    attachment
to you
    my one and only
who I let go
when I walked out that day
in late May
why this one choice
eats me alive
    inside out
the most
all-encompassing devouring pain
that will not fade
it wakes with me
rests with me
walks and talks with me
seeps into my being.

with me, always
like you
kinda
sorta.

Jim White

NOT HERE

Everywhere I look
there you are
yet
invisible
a touch
      once there
      now gone
like eyes closed, visualize
the smooth skin, that warm cozy scent
just out of the shower
as my nose dips into your neck

everywhere I go
you are absent
yet present
in my heart
on my tongue
over my mind space

why can't I just delete?
erase like chalk
old letters
burned up in ash

yet here I am
      still
      will
      power
      fading
      outstretched
      to you

      not in view.

HOW MUCH?

Never did I know
how much
the heart could ache
and how much
a lung would
quake

I didn't wanna find out
but its inevitable
for all
          on some level
exploding into millions of pieces
cells, species, creations, blades of grass

this heart can withstand a storm
but how much
          is beyond
          our grip
          on
          reality
          as we
          believe
          we are breaking
          completely.
          how much more
          until there's nothing
          solid
          left?

The heart becomes
a beat in tune
with the winds, flames and waves
invisible to all
except the third eye

Jim White

raised
above.

A PHOTOGRAPH NEATLY PLACED
INSIDE A WORN-DOWN WALLET

I've heard it said
that true love expects nothing
in return

hard to grasp

but now
I get it

throughout my body
within, without
I love
with no word
returned

the irony is
I'm alone

it's true
I let her go
yet I carry her with me
like a photograph neatly placed
inside a worn-down wallet.

Jim White

WE MAY PASS EACH OTHER

We are far out
        gone
but only a few miles apart
no matter where our feet
stand
hang or rest

we may pass each other
on the thruway,
grabbing a coffee
filling the gas tank

We were 'it'
        and now we are out, up, around
        beyond repair

        end
        or is it
        some twisted new
        beginning
        a reinvention, reincarnation, restoration
        of us

don't you wonder
        if there was some sort of
sign
from
above?

Butterfly, rainbow, hailstorm, maelstrom

        maybe today,
        we will pass
        each other.

THE LEAK IS FULL BLOWN

When there's just
one
in a field of millions

full bloom
a lone purple rose
stands apart
a force that tugs
        at your
dart
strings
these wings,
wish to soar
        but the floor
        grips
        and you fail
        to speak
        or seek
        the leak is full blown
        in a sense
        grown
        only veering off track
        further
        from
        the one
        still near
        while simultaneously
        so far off.

3:33

I dreamt of you last night
we layed together
I kissed tears on your cheeks

When I woke it was 3:33
I rolled over and found
a cold watch

if only I could find you
that way
        in my bed
as I roll over.

Who knew
the day to day routines
would be sketched inside heart speak
with such precision
and lingering longing

Clarity without hope
but a tiny percent
that maybe
        someday
        the dream
        becomes real
as I roll over on you
at 3:33.

THE FORCE OF ALL

How do you stop
this love?

Is it obsession?
A fantasy built up in the sandcastles of the mindspace.

How
    do you stop
this craving, yearning?

an army of ants devour a potato chip.

How
    do you stop
this overwhelming
    undeniable
    desire
from taking me
    under
    ground
    under water
the force of all
 back
to the original
    state
    of
    one.

THE FLIP SIDE PHOTO ALBUM OF NOSTALGIA

I dream about you
it's true
in all seasons
at all hours
is there rhyme or reason?
Possibly
      as the thunderstorm rolls in
      to spin
our daze into
hazy
recollection
the flip side photo album
      of nostalgia

a clear direction
      with no time-frame
a shame
      blanket
like car grease
eventually wears off
just after you've given
      up

life gets the final crack
      one last laugh
as you sip your morning coffee
that first magnificent taste
      and wonder
how many more
      are there?

IN FINITE MIND

Turn
      over
tumble
      OFF
beds
      grass
      concrete steps
      brain waves
      rolling thunder
      under
      the weight of it
      ALL
      down the hall
      she goes
an extraordinary creature
      back to you
fading
      black
      blue
      through
      zoomed-in view
      to taste
      one
      final
      orgasm
      IN finite
      mind.

Jim White

TO WANDER AIMLESSLY

in the maze
of love
gone

Detour
that road tipped
sideways
like mindframe
torn open
to be re-paved
u-turn bottle neck
last call
last breath
imagined daily
like some moaning wild animal
on a full moon in September
crushed cans
in hands
like stones
with glass full of sand
counting
down
ways
a play
today
the haze
no longer raising
to wander aimlessly
in the daze
of love
gone
forever lost and
found.

EVERY DAY, EVERY WAY

ALL
I
      want
      see
      dream of
      crave
      regret
      need
      yearn for
      reach to
      wish for
      lost
      is
      you.

All
of
you
and me
ALL
      of us
all
      the time
all
      the way
all
over
all day
every   day
      every   way.

ROLL OVER & THROW MY
LEG ON TOP OF YOU

Traffic hissing through the window
I thought it was classical music
      distorted
on my clock radio

dreams of you, again
real life crawls
like earthworm on pavement
if only I could roll over
and throw my leg on top
of you
smell you one more time
      just one more

but it is never enough,
this love
like glove, we want to
      grip
      eternally
in a graceful overhead floating
      like the owl
      in open space, free

      we flee
      and climb trees
      for views
      anew
yet slipping backwards
in memory bank
to tap into
      the universal dew.

WE COULD SLOW DANCE ENDLESSLY

Is it madness
      sadness
running for soul
chasing a tail
that doesn't exist

maybe headless mating call
in daylight
is the key

It's the madness
      sadness
like tiny bubbles at the surface
      popped
dropped
under
dreamscape
as fate escapes
in eyes frozen with
heart reflections
that trip on wet leaves
by the pond
      your hand broke
      if only we spoke
      just a little
      more
this madness, sadness
wouldn't stand a chance
we could slow dance
in the kitchen
      endlessly.

Jim White

THE VIBE OF YOU

Those eyes
those deep blue ocean eyes
I would give all I am to look
       into
those magic spells again

those hands
with the touch of
healing
love
       desire

your laugh echoes in my daydreams
your voice quietly lulls me to sleep
your thighs
       where my head aims to go
       deep
your lips slowly, softly pull mine
in
the vibe of you
       your presence
       upon my mind
       bones
       my beyond
       this world space, place, face
       in front of mine
       one more
       time
       in universal
       rhyme.

INFINITE LIGHT AT THE END

of the funnel cloud

Sacrifice
entice
cannonball off the peace bridge
a wake
awakening
darkening
harkening
covered up on hot sticky leather couch
a bundle
a mess
a mumble
before bed
    off
    into transformation dimensions
maybe, just
maybe
to return
    again
and when
I see your face
the only one of billions, in focus
    infinite light at the end
    of the funnel
    cloud
    just
    passing through
for you.

I'VE FALLEN UNDER

There's no drug strong
     enough
No punch hard
     enough
No time long
     enough
no megaphone loud
     enough
no miracle cure quick
     enough
no victory sweet
     enough
no success story big
     enough
no fling or string can satisfy
no amount of prayers can cure
no hobby or passion deep
     enough
no drink intoxicating
     enough

to drown out
     this voice
     reason
     yearning
     season
     I've fallen
     under.

WHY I FIND YOU

Leaves dip and dive in the country side
never
      another
      one
      like you
me
us
gone, yet here
far off
yet
substance
into blood
or breath
under flood
      of
      the question
      why
      I
      find
      you
again and again
      mystery unfolding
because you are the one
rare
      soul
      creature
so far
away
      a day
      light
      saving
      play
      on

Jim White

lines
where words dance
in rays
of
release.

A SIGN

I am nostalgia embodied
You were running
down at the small-boat harbor
you hated sweating
with that bandana on your head
a drip of sweat trickled down your cheek

rucking through the deep woods, reminiscing
I came across a girl running
bandana on dome, sweating
reminded me of that day
fantasies, visions, delirium
suddenly
a white butterfly fluttered over my head
a sign
but what?

I ask the insects, trees and cardinals...

drinking undertow
        nightly
pages melt into places
        gulping strong elixirs to try and slow
        it
        down
you know
        here and now
        is a madness evolved state
        nostalgia
        just a temporary
        escape.

THAT FIRST AND LAST MOMENT

Spiral-bound memories
hose water thirst
a baseball kept in shape
in a case
the place was safe
you and I had
      all
      we needed
      until I threw it away
      a tidal wave that has kept pace
      ever since.

Each day is another
reminder
shuffling the deck
in brain lanes
throwing blankets on the floor
      that first and last moment
      you cross my mind

walking in and out of my dream
like shadows on the wall
      candles blown out
      small puffs of smoke drift
      recycled calendars
      bottom of fire pit
      faces blend
      into the great wide open
      where I
      wander
      wondering
      when
      we will see
      again.

THE WAY

It's in the way
      you move

the way
      you speak

in the way
      you lay on the couch

the way
      you blow dry your hair

in the way
      you say my name

the way
      you look at me in bed

in the way
      you walk into the house in your black fleece and blue scrubs

the way
      you squeeze me when we hug

in the way
      you moan and say "oh my god"

the way
      you twirl your hair while driving

in the way
      you slide your frozen feet under my warm legs

the way
      you look at me when we slow dance

in the way
      you still ride my vibe
      even though I am here

Jim White

you are there
these places
that someday will no longer be
faces
blurred under car wash foam brushes.

HER CURLS WRAPPED IN HER FINGERS

Crazy is
      what
      they say
Warrior or worrier
mindset or mindflow
      release and allow the waves
      to come and go
maybe you are too much
for any and every one

      But
      the ONE
      you let go
Lo and behold
she's in your film reels again
before they turn into a broken record nightmare,
close your eyes and imagine
      she's in your room
      and all is perfect
      in the universe

Rising

in a word beyond language
      falling free
      like leaves
      twirling
      her curls wrapped in her fingers
      oh to be them..

RUBBING HANDS OVER THIGHS

If I could taste one flavor
for the rest of my days
it would be you
my favorite meal
I miss
    on a level like Himalayan mountain bliss
    more than any quick
    fix
    the gift
    that blooms
    every single second
    in this temporary trip
    into eternity

you are a sunny day in the sand
with soothing waves
    rubbing hands over thighs
    like the tides
    in and out
    perfectly aligned.

POST-IT NOTES

I write you love letters
     not every day
as that would be too much to bear
but the words come
often
like the post-it notes you left
when you were out of town
     hidden in my books, dressers, under the pillows

It became crucial that I express
while letting go of the
desire

to love
without needing anything in return

and who, beyond the source of all that is created
can say
what may
     come?
And what may
     flow
to design these letters to you
     even if
     I never send them
     or show.

REMNANTS

Where
are you
but
in the clouds
remnants
floating memories
I walk inside a fog
of you

every
damn
day.

JUST LIKE T-SHIRTS

I still wear the t-shirts you bought me
they fit best
just like you
don't worry I won't toss them
even if the colors fade
only a few possessions I keep
as I wander here and there
from ocean to desert to cabin in the woods
somehow someway my love will traverse
the cosmos
to your heart.

I can only wonder
if you will open the curtain
just a little
enough to touch
let it pour out

while the source of waterfalls
is busy creating galaxies
we can hop on the horse and buggy
to Savannah or Charleston
as time and distance
are no match for us.

Jim White

I'D GO SO FAR AS TO KNEEL

Those unique elements
     you thought were flaws

     sacred in my eyes

as memories go back and meet up
     with the current vibrations
no longer is it
     then
     but now
     still
all your demons
I wish to kiss

wrap my arms on you and hold tight
like stiff bark around tree trunk

I'd go so far as to kneel
     I never thought it was possible
     surreal
and yet here I am
     yearning for your feel
     again

like the seed in soil
aches
for the sun
and the rain.

LIKE A MOVIE

We met at spot coffee
You had on those big black boots and dark blue jeans
I loved watching you move towards me
carrying your hot tea
something in your motion
      seeped into me
      sensations I have never felt since

The past floats in and out of brain cells, so strange
      like watching the sunset
      joy in the moment
      sadness that it's ending
      hungry for more

and we have faith that the dawn will come
again
tomorrow
but will I see you walking towards me that way
once more?

What would I say?
The day I play
in mind
      like an independent film
      somewhat obscure
      yet as true as this heart
skipping
      a beat
      jump rope like
      it leaps.

THE DOG SIGHS

Her legs up on the chair
as I cut the lawn
she's nonchalant, reading magazines
I'm focused on the line
trying to get it straight
the lawnmower gets closer to her
I lean in
that soft kiss that says
hi
you and me babe
the dog sighs
we go back to our worlds.

THANKS FOR THE DREAMS

There's a fine line
      I've learned to walk it well
if only it led you back to me

They say I gotta be grateful
      for what I have

So I say thanks
for the dreams
      you keep showing up in

it's the only way I can
      see
      touch
      taste
      feel
      be near
      you.

I'll walk that line
      between reality and imagination
      where art meets invisible essence meets metamorphosis meets beauty
      meets stinging pain of absence eventually transformed
      like butterfly
      into fantasy
      come true.

CALENDAR

Check out this model, he said
I looked at the magazine cover
        She's nice, but
    it's kinda like that free calendar
    that came with the newspaper
bland, generic
no photos, no art
it doesn't light you up inside

compared to the calendar you proudly display on the kitchen wall
twelve months of big, bold creative images
each page you hold in your hand
mindfully
admiring the photography, colors, composition

like my love
she's the whole package
        twelve months that spark me inside and out
        she is nature and muse
        harmony and flow
        the sunflower glow

I told her I could wait until the end of time
for this love is a flame
flickering
eternal.

IT'S BEEN POURING OUT

Drunk dial
Sober awhile
hammered text
straight letters
walking the yellow line balance beam
and the highlights are blinding
0333 thoughts
1533 yearnings
it's a 24-7-365 unquenchable thirst

how do I shut the valve off?
        The flood keeps rising
        it's been pouring out
        of me
        for what may be
        centuries.

It's been days, hazy
weeks, crazy
months, blazin
years, a raging storm
since I've seen you
in the flesh
yet I still desire
just as much
if not more
for I've realized
        true love
        knows zero limits.

Jim White

WORK OF ART

How do you look at a work of art?

As a whole
or
at the details
piece by piece, corner to corner
zoom in and out

Like how I see you, my love
        all of you, one unified canvas
        then I go down
        to the specifics
        tracing with my fingertip mind
        every inch
        the moments
        stories
        this here and now heartbeat

        your legs, strong and smooth
        hands that feel and heal
        your eyes, like looking into a pristine body of water
        that moan- a roar of pleasure

        your laughs, each of them
        the all-out body-shake hysterical laughter
        the quick jolt of sudden giggles
        the subtle everyday chuckle
        all of them
        seemingly random splattered like acrylic paint
        perfectly balanced

        in the frame.

THE ONLY LIPS

A tall heavy collection of books
overflowing from the shelves
to the carpet
        my prized possessions
        until
        an ash landed on my sleeve
        a burn hole shook me into a new fire dance

        thousands of pages, I gave away
        to open my arms
        for new love

She had a chocolate lab
and quotes on the walls
        stay no go, she said
the
        only words
        I should have carved into the ceiling
        to read every day
as I rise and fall
        from the only bed
        I'll ever miss
and the only lips
        I yearn
        to kiss.

A SINGLE TEARDROP

slipping down
a cheek of infinity

We walked by the cemetery and waterfall
one of our first dates
you told me the story of your middle name
moments you never forget
etched in mind
like initials carved into a freshly poured concrete driveway.

I knew you were different
there was something pure
vibes on another level
I didn't grasp all the details of the tale
& now
I haven't seen
touched
heard
or felt you
in so long
but the images and film reel footage still
matter
as you're the only one
who lit me up
this way

and who is it I speak of?
Is it a woman on Earth or some goddess from Greek mythology?

Wandering through this great big star
spinning in one of the can't-quite-touch skies

or a force of the ancient mystics
sent from the first pages
of the first book
zipped down to the cracked planet

      from on high
      like jolt of lightning.

Maybe all in one
      as unique snowflake synchronicity
      soaring in flight like hawk at dinner
a pop art carbon copy
chunk of salt blending in
with the souls and shadows streaming along
fish-like
towards the great big sea

like a single teardrop
      slipping down
      a cheek of infinity.

BUT WHY

can't I just glide?

I said to her
maybe there's something wrong with me
why can't I just be
satisfied
normal
grateful?

Is it my fate to embrace this
repetitive
sandpaper rubbing against the palms
of my hands and face?

Where will you go? She asked

I'd live in my truck if I had to
the desert was calling me
some primitive wandering urge
aboriginal
primal union
my essence with that of the animals and landscape
connecting dots like stars in universal vines
but why
can't I just glide
like rocking chair on summer porch
laid back daze
for those recollections to raise
how close I am to your heart
again I awake and start
this stream dream
with eyes open
a saguaro cactus appears
out of the wall
as nothing is

what it seems.

SOMETHING DEEPER

Seconds
clocks
winding
clicking
blinking
breaking
back
     forward
     frozen
without the only thing that keeps
the pace:
you.

Is it need or want?
Maybe both
     or something beyond human urges

crawling in a a deserted mirage
     I need water
     I want shade
yet something deeper
     I still crave.

EVEN WHEN NO ONE IS LISTENING

They got sick of me talking about you
I couldn't turn it off
I tried
I sure did try
so hard
to get over
IT
but you know me
I don't operate like other machines
I'm more reptile, than xerox

I tried deep dives into
booze
pot
family
talking it out
parties
working until physical exhaustion
long hikes in the woods
nothing cured this drowning

in fact, every attempt to escape the truth
made it worse

then it hit me
like forehead to a steering wheel

I began to write
an ode
to the love of my life
the most rare creation of
letters, images, memories, words, dreams, flesh, blood and
beyond

Jim White

just like you.

maybe a few people
       get it
it matters
not
as the bird sings
       even when no one is listening.

CLIMB THE MOUNTAIN AND HOWL AT THE MOON

The last time I was in the Adirondacks
you and I
we
a thing
legit
substance
that dissolved
        even now, dissipates
yet remains
        solid
in some strange
        dimension of mind current

I'm headed back
alone

but you travel with my heart
still

What can I do?
Climb the mountain
        and howl at the moon.

Jim White

UNDERWATER DREAM

I left you
found a void
one that can never be filled
        only your presence can soothe the demon
I tried with all the heavy hitters
        windmills
        naval fleets
        hurricanes
        floods
        one thousand tanks
        avalanche
        nothing can fill
the empty space I found
when I ran, gasping for air

Can't escape
Have to face the cold concrete barricade
        daily
        until
        one day
        I'll awake
and see your bright eyes
looking into mine
        even if
        it's an underwater dream.

TAKING IT OFF

If only I knew
      what I was seeking
was not mind FULL
      but mind LESS

we could be laying together right now

taking it off
      instead of
      putting it on

when my masterpiece is
complete
I'll dedicate it
      to you my dear
      as you created it
I just put pen to paper.

If there's no
you and I
I'm on a mission to delete
me

before you freak out, dear reader
it's poetry
transformation
elevation
      like
      raven's wings outstretched fully
      free
      to see
      and not be,

      clearly

what comes

from this hand
I can't say
just as nightmares unfold
without my input

now I can only burn
like thick logs in the midnight trance
staring into the blue, yellow and orange flames

speaking
another language
can you hear?
the message is clear

let's take it off
knock these walls down
break through
and put on the white gown.

MYSTERIOUS OCEAN

Why is she the ONE?

The mysterious ocean
you don't have to understand
but if you do
      you've felt the sublime
      beyond human logic
      transcendence.

One more time
      in the ocean
      at the park
      walking the sidewalks at night
      on a road trip
      in a log cabin
      on the carpet
      feet in the sand
      head in the clouds
      sharing a beer
      or peanut butter pie
      together
      one more time
      swimming in the mysterious ocean.

IN A DRYER SPINNING CHAOTIC LAND

If there was one
who could say my name and
I'd crawl out of the cave

just one

it's you
no one else can penetrate this wall
only you
and I can wait
forever
and beyond that too.

you are everything I've ever wanted
in a woman
even if we don't speak
weak
in the knees
it's still the only story that makes
sense
in a dryer spinning chaotic land
you and I can swim
in peace
under the full moon
of a word
that we know
yet often
hold back
it flies above
grips like glove
rhymes with dove
and hits like a brick.

REAL FUNNY

It's like the great joke
        from above
I find the essence of love
and she's gone

my heart has grown
        and blown
        apart
I laugh and shout to the sky
        are you high?!
Funny thing is
        I'm not sad or lonely

Alone, yes
        I inhale all the emotions
        and breathe them out
        just the same

the edge spoke to me
crawling in the dark
        handed me a key
to be
        this wild roaming human creature
        yet still desire the one I love
        in some sort of strange peace
between worlds

without her,
        I'm called to the woods
there's no other
only the trees, rocks, snakes and rivers

a rare creature may relate
It's out of my hands
        & my mind.

Jim White

DEAR SOUL MATE

We are forever connected

yet here and now
		the phone line is dead

on this level
I can't reach you
kiss you
lay on top of you

I know other levels, morse code, smoke signals, SOS

 but dear,

help me reconcile
I've got my compass out

I know you feel it
still
true north
lines up your heart and mine

we are both looking up at the same sky
I'll nudge you with my elbow

hey babe,
let's watch the milky way together
on the grass
in our favorite blanket
I'll bring a fun beer
everything crystal clear.

BONFIRE

A stranger asked me:
Who is this girl you write about?
She must be special

I smile and nod
the most extraordinary woman I've ever known
she's a nurse
but there's no title that can define her

words aren't enough
but I'll give you a hint

Her middle name
     builds
     my bonfire.

SIMPLE

All I want
        is to lay in a tent
        with you
and listen to thunderstorms
        for hours
        days
        a hundred thousand years

forget the world
        and listen
        to your thunder

just once more
        and know
the night
is ours
to savor.

CHECK, MATE

I've come across
        many stubborn people
Yet I
        was always the king
until my love came along

if you play chess, you know the queen
is the most powerful piece
across the board
the king can only rule
        in his own perimeter

ironically, one of the greatest feats in life
to conquer ones own hell

even as the queen
        puts you in check
        mate.

THE BUTTERFLY SINGING
ON THE SUMMIT

What is love but
    a song that makes you feel good
    for three minutes

What is love but
    a four letter word
    that conjures images of bubbly little red hearts

What is love but
    wine and dine and fine line
    walking together with a stuffed animal
    in kind

What is love other than
    a song that hurts when you hear the first verse

What is love other than
    a four letter word that rhymes
    with
    buck

What is love other than
    an idea manufactured by movie producers
    that leaves you hanging

But wait a momet

listen..

    I've heard a whisper in the ocean's surf
    the frost pine, sap drizzle
    and the butterfly singing on the summit

Love is found
    when you no longer seek

and ask
for nothing
no gifts or praise
expecting no words of affection

you'd give all of your self
and it matters not what comes
back
for love is beyond
a word or concept
bumper sticker or holiday card cliche

it comes unexpectedly
when you throw away
every conception
ever
thrust
in your perception.

SNAPSHOT

We reached the summit
    of our first mountain together
there's a picture to prove
it's not purely nostalgia
    peek in
    the peak moment
    for I speak to spark
    a transformation within
    yet without the clock
    that cabin in the woods
    on the lake
    some memories never fade
    but drift slowly
    like sand dune
    alive and
    well.....

    arrived
    and
    hell
    if I know
    why
you're the one forever tattooed
    on my wild naked human soul
and you know me
    I was born to roll
    solo
yet there's a glimmer like
    serenity
    on that lake
    reflecting back a moveable
    snapshot
    of every minute
    with you.

ONE LAST RIDE

Thought I knew love
    really I did

but it was a revelation
    that only came after loss
    a dance with the devil
    and a walk down the plank

Swimming to shore
with wisdom to share
    barking at the moon

    I get it now!

Without a human near
    like a tree falling in the dusk
but hey
    maybe she feels my vibe
a few miles away
    as I dream of
one
last
ride.

A DATE WITH FATE

How do you know
    with one hundred percent certainty
    that she is
    the one?

Spend over a year apart
close your eyes
imagine bumping into her
at some random place

unexpected date with fate

what do you feel?

Heart rate like foot slamming on the accelerator
stomach like mixing concrete
roller coaster about to drop straight down
hairs on neck stand straight up
sweat forms on your temples
hands tingly
mind digging around
    in an old dresser drawer
desperately searching for
    the right words

you've never felt this overwhelming absolute takeover
of your entire being
    with anyone else
    and never will.

AN OUTLINE OF CHALK

The green bird said:
      "love is a dangerous game"

just as I was about to ask why,
she swooped over the garage
crashing into a telephone pole
wings twitching on the sidewalk
a song suddenly
silent

beside the motionless body,
an outline of chalk
and the words:
      "it's worth it, when she's the one"

suddenly, the wise old bird
      burst
      into flight
soaring
up
into the blue
as if she wasn't just laying on
      death's door
      a moment before.

SWIMMING

For over a year
I was drowning
and couldn't get to shore

I was so close
        to done
I had no choice
        but to find
my way

creation
a book
take the pain and turn it
into a work of art

I'm swimming now
front crawl, backstroke, butterfly
at peace
        almost
        with life, death, loss

I still want
        ALL
        of her
        every day
        but
        I'm able to absorb and consume
        knowing I
        am not
        this body
        or this mind
        the emotions
        or the thoughts

 I can step back, above, below, aside

&
      breathe, dance, swim, climb, crawl
taste the delicious desire
& possibility
while
simultaneously
      not needing it
      to survive.

NOT A TRICK OR A FIX

One question remains
It's imperative you dig it up
  ask it in the mirror
with feet on edge
   the heavy weight of irony on your
   dome and foam
   without the necessity of an
   answer
for she is my question and answer
   not a trick or fix
   pure as the sticks
keeping the blaze
aflame

it comes to you
when you are ready.

AS I LET THIS PERSON
CALLED JIM GO AWAY

looking back at my 41 years
most of it a
      rumbling, yearning, recklesss, roaring
      wandering, moaning tear through the wild bush, fenced yards
      and asphalt chaos

but
      those years with her
they were the only respite
a calm before
      and after
      storms
that I find
      inside
      and all around
      I recall
      with fond memory
      melancholy
      regret
      and appreciation
as I let this person called Jim
      go away
      far
a   way

I crave
you
      now and then

who am I kidding?

You
      I crave

Jim White

ALL
ways.

TIE-DYE TSHIRT AND LOOSE
BLUE SCRUB PANTS

Meet me
  just once more
  in your old tie-dye tshirt
  and loose blue scrubs

so I can caress
  and kiss
  every
  single
inch
  of
  you
while
  dropping
  the clothes
  to the floor
  like letting go
  of past aches pains and stains.

AND GO

How did you
　　　　penetrate my psyche
　　　　and douse my heart
　　　　with your everything
　　　　like I once did
　　　　to you.

I may leave
　　　　everything
　　　　behind
but
　　　　if I had one piece of substance to take with me
　　　　it would be the green t-shirt you got me
　　　　from San Diego
　　　　I'll never forget
As I go wild, naked and free
　　　　wrapped only in that cotton size large

　　　　drifting
　　　　sifting
　　　　off
　　　　intoxicating
　　　　distant sands, shifting lands..
far out
man
gone
trippin
like
fast-forward and reverse flip flop on timeline
obliterated in paradox
like when
I'd leave before the sun
　　　　was up.
Coffee.

Take the pup outside
Watch the rabbit run
last moment
a kiss to your forehead
let's do that
again.
And go.

LOST

and
> found

Stay no go
> a story of
> love and loss
> and lost love
> love lost
> found love
> lost and found
> after all
> is
> lost
> found love lost love
> the great irony
> hear the laughter up
> in the clouds

hold on
> to me
> as I reunite
> with your essentials
> and we float
> for however long
> it takes
> as we bake
> in the summer sun.

JUST CALL ME TIMBER

Trees are my jam
    like you my dear
I'll climb
    on
    top
    under
    morning
    noon
    twilight
    hours that are
    ours
    just call me
    timber.

Each chapter
    a part of you I miss

from feet to calves to thighs
    hips
    working upwards
    and down
    whispering into ear
    kissing
    & breathing
    on your neck.
When you know
    all you want

clarity is shocking
    and the pain is precise
when she is not
    in your hands, arms or mouth.

ONE MORE MUG FULL

It's like waiting for the old coffee pot
        to brew
a slow trickle
        waiting for you
wondering if it's time
        will the pot break
        or give
        one more mug full
        and you question
        if you should release
        the hook, line
        and sink
        in your brain

        am I insane?
We all are
        in our own peculiar ways
        we just choose the details
        to cover the madness in
        pretty colors.

FLOWERS & GRAPES

A dozen roses I never did see
      the first time I ever ordered
      a rainbow
they delivered to your doorstep
yet I have no idea
      if you placed them in a vase
      or the garbage bin
      if you smiled or cried
      or burned them alive

regardless
      I'd do it again
because I've found
      love gives
      like open hands
      never closing in for a
      return

but wait a minute,
she loves cotton candy grapes..

I'm asking the clouds above and below
      How can I grow these?
      Maybe
      I can entice her
      to enter
      my grape grove

for real
heal
the deal
of a life
time
no shaking hands necessary

Jim White

grape in mouth
hands still
open
wide.

UNTIL THE SUN OPENS EYES AGAIN

Why is it
    clarity only comes
    from destruction

cardboard torn apart
crumbling foundations into flooded rivers
rock bottom
the absolute certainty
to realize
only when
it's gone
    miles away
out of touch
out of reach
out of fucking control
    and yet
the crickets are chirping to
the birds

chill
come listen with me
I'll massage you down
all hours

ours to revel in
    until the sun opens eyes again.

RUNNING LATE

There is only one
name
      face
      heart
      soul
      mate
      fate
      date
      maybe we are just running
      late.

MILES

It's true
      kind of blue
got me through
      like
breaking
new
      ground
      I found
sounds
but lost
      you
flames in lanes gone
      awry
to get high
      a temporary peak
      fully immersed
      in the elation
      followed by desperation
      for one follows
      right after
      the other.

A painting of language
      a direct result of your
      very
      existence

Maybe the message will resonate
      it's out of my power
I didn't choose these creations
      they came
      to me
when I tuned in

Jim White

invitations
        to
        intuitions
        instinctive
a vision
        flickering candle light in the dark
        hall
to be revealed
for the world to consume
all because you were born
my dear
Kashka.

SURRENDER

becomes
salvation

Standing on cracked driveway
    inhaling smoke from pine and maple
    still
    as the lone star above
    amidst shifting clouds
formed
and
formless
    just the same
wondering
    how
I can get through
    to you
the only true
desire
had me at the edge of
the abyss
powerless
    floating without air
grasping at tree branches
invisible
    just out of reach
surrender
    becomes
    salvation.

FOREST AND FIRE AND
POEM AND PAINT

Without you
      there's nothing for me
      but the woods
      and creation

With you
      forest and fire and poem and paint

Some are born to wolves and moonshine
some are torn by doves and sunrise

with or without

it's forest
fire
poem
paint

offered up this flesh image
to
the bears
snakes
and
mountain lions

maybe the spirits have one last dance
planned
for
us
before
they take me

      to become
mud

honey
moss
running
water.

STANDING TALL

Time does not heal all wounds
You just learn to adjust your
        position
like a throbbing pain in the shoulder
you roll over

until you find a spot
that doesn't hurt as much

joy and despair share the same
stick
I wish I could flip
like magic trick

a heart with our initials
carved into an oak tree

the shape of her
        thighs
        eyes
        lips
        fingers
        neck line
        I stand tall
        before
        her.

SHATTERED GLASS BECOMING BRICKS

Purple heart
dripping teardrop
into a deep pond
the ripples spread out
in rings
turning into an ocean wave
becoming a drip of
     sweat
blending into another purple heart
exploding
     into hundreds of tiny pieces
shattered glass
     becoming bricks
in a wall
     with the words
     Stay no Go
     appearing like ghosts

     a cactus poking up
     out of the brick wall

     love and loss and lost love can never be
     love
     it's found
     a ways off.

Jim White

THE ONE WHO KNOWS

what he wants

Every phrase
quote
idea
book
bumper sticker
motivational slogan
platitude
optimistic lingo
mean
nothing
to the one
who knows
what he wants

yet
can only close his eyes
and visualize
as she is gone
off
but only
a few minutes away.

LIKE MY TRUCK?

You told me to check out this song..

Like my truck? I asked.

Yes.
But more than that

If I was to ride anywhere
just the two of us
cruising down the highway
to the mountains
beaches
woods
your hand in mine
nothing else
        on my mind

until we both pull away
and I grip your thigh
we never liked holding hands anyway.

HOME

Bruises on my legs and arms
       sore in places rarely touched
just what I needed
satisfaction of physical labor
sweat, dirt, exhaustion

I'm not meant for the shirt and tie
office life

I'm a wild man
chopping wood, hiking, crawling by day
writing, painting and howling by night

swimming nude in the ocean
I'll go
all day
disappear into the darkness
crash in the sand
with ghost crabs running on my sandy limbs

If I don't have her to come home to
I'd rather not go home
      at all.

730 DAYS

You once thanked me
      for the best
      730 days of your life

Now I see how the script
      flips
      dips
      and trips
      under
      the weight
      of the worst
      730 days of my life
      since I left.

NOW JUST A SONG

Regardless
        if I like it or not
seasons play out
without a fast forward or rewind button
a house built on stilts
        over an earth, alive
        shifting

even if we approve
        or dislike
the leaves will fall
        crunching under foot
        eyes peer down
        as if seeing
        for the first time

regardless
        if I like it or not
we are here
        then gone

she and I were
        now
        just a song.

TO CLEAR THE WAY

Everyday I wake up
laying on a new sword

I spend hours pulling it out
carefully at first
then aggressive
         desperate to clear the way
for another
         ray
         of light.

when maybe
         the sword
         won't dig so deep
         and maybe
         we will meet and peek
         into our next chapter
         a story of magic
         we take the leap
         inside.

COMES AND GOES

I used to despise the fall season
so did she

we joked about pumpkin spice and foliage
while everyone obsessed about it

and now
        I am indifferent

        weather
comes and goes
        just like all of us

there's no high or low
worth taking sides over

without her,
        it's a day, week, month, season
        passing by
        as it did
        before
         and after
        we were here

 ready for the final curtain call
        or credit roll
        in the dry desert sun

        as my life fades to dusk
        behind the mighty saguaro cactus.

A MIRAGE

Mind sway
heart silenced
gut ignored

      instinct knows
yet I walked
away
oblivious
seeking a mirage
and instead
      sinking into a dungeon of regret

our potential metamorphosis
      at peak
like crouching deep
      before the giant
      leap.

HER LINGO

She had her own language
I entered the fray
we blended our words
like oil and vinegar
        stirred up
        and drizzled
        on a bowl of fresh greens
        our day by day themes
        extraordinary as a pair

even now, apart
her lingo remains
a rare phenomenon

just as she
        is my
        lone rose
        poking up above the weeds.

We had our own code
likely indecipherable

missers
funky feelers

lady in white

so clear
yet so distant
from what the brain stem
considers
tangible
to bloom
once
again.

WHAT ELSE IS THERE TO DO?

We didn't split for the usual reasons
>nothing about us
>or IT
>her
>or me
>is or was
>normal

you won't get it
>but she did
>yet
>it blows
>I can't fix it
>or start anew

>instead
>I write a book about it

create
paint the silence
conjure the imagery
>out of sorrow and distress

what else is there to do?

Jim White

A DEEP RIVER

People see my desire
the unrelenting inexplicable passion
the absolute obliterating love
for you
and they are amazed and curious
they want to know more
more, more
it's never enough
I concur, I need more too

why how when where?

your love is so deep, they say
so sincere
so serious
why can't I have that in my life?

And yes I admit, it's a deep river,
FULL of life
but also
a sledgehammer to the heart
brain and gut

but I don't try and change it
even if it destroys
this self I see
in the rearview
as I wipe the glass clean.

WAVES

It's no longer crashing
against the break wall
but now
bobbing at the surface
I send love
no need to catch
I want it
but no longer need
like a junkie with sleeves up

the destructive storms have given way

calm waves
lapping against the shore.

THE SURF

She said
love
always
      miss
forever
      never
forget
      it was the best
with me
      indeed.

will the surf wipe the memories
      away

      today
      or tomorrow
      or
      will they become permanent
      in the universal
      sea salt

Someday
I will

Find

Out

End
Begin
A new.

TUCK YOU IN

When I first stayed the night
you had to work early
I would tuck you in and stay up

quietly, I'd nuzzle
against your warm body
arms around you
or hand on hip

the bed was against the wall, where you liked it
sometimes I'd stay,
sometimes I'd go

after awhile I didn't want to leave
a new world opening up

it's a strange life
when you look back
     an instant later you are present
that fantasy is gone
& you wonder
how we made it happen
yet can't
find it again
like the old snowblower that won't start up
only trouble is
no mechanic can fix this malfunction
     you're in one bed
     I'm in another.

MAYBE JUST ONCE MORE

What started as a joke

a phrase
        one and done

words blur with multiple meanings

in the shower
on vacation
the only time
a combination of
pleasure
delicious nostalgia
and
yearning
lack
desiring
melancholic memory
for there was only
one
and
done

but hey
we did it right
we made some light
in a world too often dark

I would break our record
and do it
maybe just once
more

and
go.

FOOTBALL

Road games
adventures
cruising across the country
to see our football team play
in other cities

jumping in lakes
floating in oceans
talking to seals
baby giraffes, tigers and rhinos
so many nights and days we played
in the woods
by the fire
on the road from Cali to Vegas
weddings, dancing
imagining
our future together..

your laughs
sighs, excitement, groans
the highs and lows,
I would never trade away
as we created memories
that linger
far beyond today.

it may hurt in ways
I still can't escape
but I'll take it in stride
knowing you and I had something profound

even though we should be
together,
creating a new story

Jim White

the past,
calm
in it's chambers
resting

the future, unknown
riding on the waves
of wonder
and wishes

we watch our team
on different screens.

DATE NIGHT

We were busy but we
made time
for date night

I have an idea that will blow those away
To give us another chance

We can be the great comeback story
        finding a way
        overcoming all odds

First, I'd bring your favorite coffee and
a fresh breakfast sandwich to you in bed

Then I'd rub you
        all the way up and down while kissing
        every part of your soft skin
        taking off your clothes, slowly
        and mine
        as we come together
        like we used to
        but this time
        the build up is like volcano

As you become totally relaxed, I put on some of your favorite music
songs we used to listen to at your cabin
cookouts and bonfires
holding you tight
laughing, reminiscing

Then we'd hop in my truck and go kayaking on the lake
summer vibes
a smooth ride
playing games on sunny days

we'd go home for the pup

take a stroll around the neighborhood
kissing your neck
laughing in the warm July night
excited about future trips and adventures

after that we'd make dinner together
slow dancing in the kitchen
forgetting about the world for awhile
just us
just love
and the dog jumping on me
to protect you

when the moon
        comes out
we ride into the country
find a quiet spot to lay our blanket down
and watch shooting stars

our folks, RIP, smiling down at us

we share stories, the moment, a future together..

        we finish the night with a hug
        that tight, holding-on-for-dear-life kind of
embrace
then a deep slow kiss
one you never want to end
&
just before closing the door
        I get down on my knee
        doing what I've never done
        asking for your hand & heart
 for eternity
 and wait for you to say:
 oh my god

 and go.

        Stay no Go.

Made in the USA
Monee, IL
19 January 2021